10

MYTHS
ABOUT DEBTS,
COLLECTION ACTIONS
AND
BANKRUPTCY
THAT EVERY CONSUMER SHOULD KNOW

The Ultimate Guide for Protecting You from Aggressive Debt Collection

EDRIE PFEIFFER
ATTORNEY AT LAW
Hampton Roads Legal Services
372 S. Independence Blvd, Suite 109
Virginia Beach, Virginia 23452
757-340-3100
www.hamptonroadslegal.com
E-mail: info@hamptonroadslegal.com

Copyright © 2012 by Edrie Pfeiffer,
3rd Printing
Hampton Roads Legal Services

All rights reserved. No part of this book may be used or reproduced or transmitted by any means, in any manner whatsoever; electronically, mechanically, photocopied, recorded or otherwise, without written permission of the author.

Printed in the United State of America.

372 S. Independence Blvd, Suite 109, Virginia Beach, VA 23452
Telephone: 757-340-3100
Fax: 757-340-3149

www.hamptonroadslegal.com

Table of Contents:

FOREWORD

Who am I and why did I write this book?

My name is Edrie Pfeiffer, and I have represented individuals in bankruptcy cases for over 15 years. During that time, my clients have told me time and time again the horror stories they have heard about debt collections and bankruptcy. These stories come from their friends and family who "know someone who had a relative that filed bankruptcy or that had this happen to them". Sometimes, despite my best efforts as an attorney, my clients believe these horror stories and make decisions based on this misinformation rather than sound legal advice.

You have done yourself a favor by requesting this book. The information that I give you in this book is designed to put you ahead of the game when it comes to collection actions and bankruptcy. All of these myths are based on actual statements that I have heard from clients over the years. As with all myths, there is a nugget of truth in them but they have been taken way out of context.

It is my hope that by reading this book, you will be better prepared to deal with collection agencies or creditors. After reading this book, you may decide that you need to have a more permanent solution to your debt problems. I hope that the chapters on bankruptcy will address any fears that you may have about the bankruptcy process.

Of course, no book can cover all the different scenarios that arise when dealing with debts. This book is not meant to be legal advice for your specific situation. In addition, this book is based on Virginia Law and the bankruptcy practices for the Eastern District of Virginia, Norfolk/Newport News Divisions. Please use this as a general guideline on dealing with debt. If you have additional questions after reading this book, please give my office a call. We will be happy to meet with you and discuss how to handle your specific questions.

Over the years, I have helped thousands of individuals escape from crushing debt loads and obtain a fresh start in life. I have also helped hundreds of individuals to stop foreclosures on their home and prevent repossession of their car. I have removed 2nd mortgages from homes that were upside down and assisted individuals who wanted to be free of a home they could no longer afford. I can do the same for you, but you have to take the first step by calling me for a consultation.

MYTH NUMBER ONE: CREDIT CARDS ARE BAD AND I SHOULDN'T HAVE ANY.

I frequently hear clients tell me that they "have learned their lesson" and they will never have a credit card again. I also see financial gurus who are always harping on how credit cards are bad and people should not have them. Somehow we have developed an attitude that a small piece of plastic is the devil's tool. The fact is that credit cards are not in and of themselves evil or destructive.

Credit Cards are a tool, and like any other tool there is nothing inherently wrong with credit cards. The problem is the way that they are used. To say that credit cards are evil is like saying that hammers are bad because people get hurt using hammers. There are a wide variety of hammers and you must use the right hammer for the job. Imagine using a sledge hammer to pound in a nail to hang a picture. Obviously this is not the right tool for the job. But that doesn't mean that all hammers are bad; you just need to have the right type of hammer.

Now if you have the right hammer for the job of pounding in the nail for the picture, you can still use the hammer wrong. Think about using the small hammer but holding the nail by the top and trying to nail it in. I can tell you from personal knowledge that this does not work. All you end up with is bruised fingers. You have to use the hammer correctly to get that nail into the wall.

The same is true of credit cards. If you have the wrong tool for the job that you are doing, you will end up in a financial mess. This, for example, is the person who claims to only use their credit cards for emergencies. While credit cards can be used for true emergencies, this can be like using the sledge hammer on the picture nail. It will work but you can end up with a mess. What happens too frequently is that you use your credit card for a true emergency like the car breakdown and then more and more things become emergencies.

A mother sent her daughter off to college with a credit card to be used only in the case of extreme emergencies. Two months later the mother got the credit card bill and the daughter had charged over $200 at the mall. The irate mother called the daughter and started to chew her out about how the card was to be used only for emergencies. The daughter interrupted and said "but Mom, this was an emergency! They had this really cute outfit on sale and the sale was ending the next day! I had to use the credit card to buy the outfit. Then I saw this darling pair of shoes that matched the outfit perfectly but they only had one pair left in my size, so I had to buy them right away."

Unfortunately, this is how many people end up using that emergency credit card. What makes things even worse is that they use the credit card for these "emergencies" and then they have to put regular household expenses on the card because they have to use their income to pay the monthly payment on the credit card. They don't have money left over to buy groceries or put gas in the car, so they put it on the credit card. Now they have a vicious cycle going with the credit card balance growing each month as they have to use it for more and more normal livingexpenses to be able to make the monthly payment.

The credit card is not to blame. They have used a sledge hammer to pound in a nail. Virtually every financial advisor will tell you that you should have an emergency fund to cover those emergency expenses like car repairs. However, it can be impossible to save money when you are caught in the cycle of charging expenses in order to make the monthly payment of the credit card. If you are caught in the this cycle, don't despair, there is a way for you to get a fresh start and break this cycle.

The second way that credit cards become evil is that they are used in the wrong way. I tell my clients that I have four credit cards that I use regularly. However I don't pay interest on the credit cards, instead they pay me to use them. All of the cards that I use are reward cards so that I get different rewards depending on the card. The only reason that I have four cards is that I have two cards that are used for my business and two cards that are used for personal use.

Most people use their credit cards to finance purchases. This is like holding the nail by the end while you are trying to hammer it in. While you might get the nail into the wall, you will end up with very sore fingers. When you use a credit card to buy something over time, you are paying far more for the item than it is worth. If you can't pay cash for the item now, you shouldn't be buying it now. Wal-Mart has started offering layaway. While they do this to make money off those people who put some money down and then never pay off the item, this is a far better option than buying the item on a credit card and then paying for it over a period of several months.

Years ago, when I got my first job and my first apartment, I had to get certain necessities like a TV. Being young and inexperienced, I went to one of those rent to own places and got a TV on a payment plan. After a couple of payments, I sat down and calculated how much I was going to pay for that TV. I was shocked to see how this TV that sold for $200 was going to cost me over $600. I returned the TV and went without until I could pay cash for one. This also applies to credit cards. If you purchase something on a credit card and make the minimum monthly payments, you will be paying for that item for several years. You may even still be paying for the item after you no longer have it.

As I stated before, I have credit cards and I use them regularly. I have one credit card that offers a rebate on gas purchases so I charge all my gas on that card and receive the rebate on the purchase. I have another card that I use to pay for all regular monthly expenses that will accept a credit card, like the phone bill and cable bill. One credit card is used for the business expenses and one credit card is used for court expenses. All of these cards offer some form of reward, whether it is points for each dollar spent or rebates for the dollars spent. Every month, when the bills come in, I write one check for each card to pay the balance in full. This saves me time and postage. I have been able to use my points to take vacations and buy Christmas presents.

is the correct way to use a credit card and helps to build your credit score.

If you have been hitting your fingers while trying to put the nail in the wall and are carrying large balances on your credit cards, don't despair. There is a way for you to get rid of those balances without having to eat ramen noodles and tuna fish for the rest of your life.

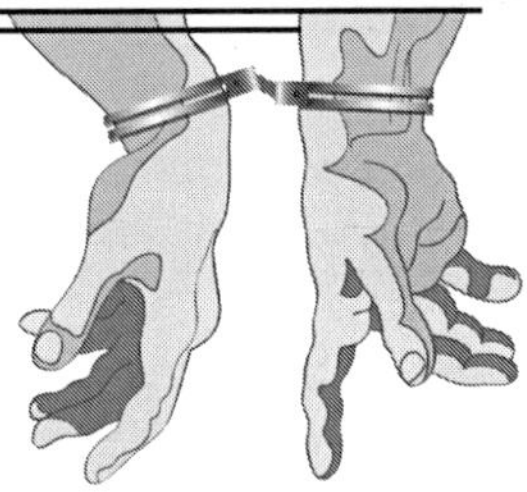

MYTH NUMBER TWO: THEY CAN ARREST ME IF I DON'T MAKE THE PAYMENTS ON AN ACCOUNT.

This is one of the worst misleading actions that I have seen by collection agencies over the past years. You receive a phone call and the person making the call is very abusive and says that if you don't make an immediate payment on this account, they will take legal action, implying that they will have a warrant issued for your arrest. In fact, recently I had a message left on my home answering machine that was extremely hostile and threatening. They had the wrong number, but I called the number that they left and chewed them out for the nature of the message that was left. While I am very familiar with the laws that control Collection Agencies, someone who is not could be very frightened by the message.

Collection Agencies must abide by the Fair Debt Collection Practices Act. This law tells Collection Agencies when they can place calls to consumers and what they can say in these calls. Collection Agencies are prohibited from making misleading or false claims. The threat to have you arrested violates both of these prohibitions. First the threat is misleading. They cannot have you arrested in Virginia for failing to pay a bill. If they file a lawsuit at all, it is normally a Warrant in Debt which is a civil action, not a criminal action. You will receive a copy of the Warrant in the mail and the sheriff will also deliver one to your door. However, the sheriff is not there to arrest you, he is simply delivering the paperwork. Depending on the amount of the debt, the Creditor may also file a Motion for Judgment in the Circuit Court. Warrants in Debt are filed in the General District Court, Virginia's equivalent to a small claims court.

If the creditor uses the form provided by the Courts, there is a notice on it that says you are not required to appear at the hearing. However if you do not appear, the creditor may get a Judgment against you. I always tell clients that a Judgment is simply a Judge declaring that you owe these people money. BIG DEAL!! You know that you owe them money, having a Judge declare that you owe them money does not change that. More importantly, the Judgment does not change the debt. You can still wipe out the debt even if they have a Judgment.

What is more important about a Judgment is that the Creditor must have a Judgment to begin involuntary collection procedures against you. I will talk more about this in the next Chapter. In addition, a Judgment is a Legal Record and will show up on your credit report. If you have a creditor that has filed a lawsuit against you, then you need to take immediate action to stop this process.

There is one thing that must be addressed about the threat to have you arrested for not making a payment, and this deals with car loans. While a creditor cannot have you arrested for failure to make a payment, I am seeing Creditors filing theft charges against individuals for car loans when they are unable to repossess the car. In one case, the Creditor had not even attempted to repossess the car. They filed the theft charge because they believed, in error, that the car had been taken out of state by the client's college age daughter. If you have a car loan that you are behind on and they tell you that they will file theft charges if you don't turn over the car, you should believe them. ***Do not try to hide the car.*** There are ways to get the car back if you must have that car. Your options after repossession are limited and very time sensitive. If you are facing a repossession or have had a car repossessed, you need to take action now.

The second way that many Collection Agencies violate the law is by telling people that they will pursue legal actions if the individual does not make an immediate payment. Many Collection Agencies have been successfully sued for claiming that they will initiate legal action when they have no record of ever filing a suit against some one. If you have a Collection Agency telling you that they will take you to court if you don't make an immediate payment, don't believe them. I always tell clients that until you actually get something from a court, this is just another collection call. If you are being harassed by collection calls, then the time to take action has come. Trying to ignore these calls is only a temporary solution. You need to eliminate the debt and stop this creditor nonsense.

A side note on the Fair Debt Collection Practices Act: It apples only to collection agencies. It does not apply to the original creditor or their employees.

MYTH NUMBER THREE: THEY WILL TAKE MY PAYCHECK OR THE MONEY IN MY BANK ACCOUNT IF I DON'T MAKE PAYMENTS.

This is another one of the misleading statements that bill collectors love to tell debtors. This threat is normally made in a threatening phone call where they also imply that they will notify your employer if you don't make an immediate payment. The truth of the matter is that while they can garnish or take a portion of your wages and the money in your bank account, they must go through a process that takes some time to complete. If you miss a payment or even a couple of payments, they cannot immediately take your paycheck or the money in your bank account, unless you have previously authorized them to take the money from your account.

When a creditor takes money from your bank account or your wages without your permission, it is called a garnishment. This is a court-ordered involuntary collection action. Before a creditor can garnish your wages or your bank account, they must first get a Judgment against you for the debt. They must attempt to serve a copy of the Warrant in Debt or Motion for Judgment on you. However, this can be done by sending it to the last address that they have for you. If you have moved since you incurred the debt, they do not have to update the mailing address that they have for you. Many times the first notice that someone gets that a creditor has gone to Court for a judgment is when their wages or their bank account have been garnished.

Many creditors are quick to take action to obtain judgments when an account is delinquent. Foremost among these are creditors for repossessed cars and furniture companies, such as Grand Furniture. Several credit card companies and medical providers also move fairly quickly to obtain Judgments and then garnishments. If you have these types of debts, you will need to take action as soon as possible to prevent the creditor from garnishing your wages or bank account.

In Virginia, once a creditor has obtained a Judgment, they must wait 10 calendar days before they can request a garnishment. When they file for a garnishment, the court will set a hearing date on the Garnishment Summons. This is not the date for the garnishment to begin but rather the date for the money to be sent to the court and turned over to the Creditor. Garnishments against wages are normally done for up to six months and garnishments against bank accounts are normally done for 90 days.

If the Creditor has started a garnishment against your wages, your employer must withhold 25% of your pay after taxes for the garnishment period up to the amount of the Judgment unless you fall below certain income levels. Normally if you are working full time, they will be able to take 25% of your pay after taxes. If the Creditor garnishes your bank account, the bank must withhold all of the money in accounts that have your name on them, and all money that is deposited in the bank during the garnishment period up to the amount of the Judgment. Most banks are not very detail oriented on this and may end up withholding or freezing more money that they should.

There are certain types of monies that cannot be garnished. However, you must prove to the Court that the money in your bank account falls into one of these exempt categories. You can find a list of the exempt categories on the back of the Garnishment Summons. If you have income from one of these categories, you must request a hearing from the Court that issued the Garnishment Summons to have the Garnishment removed from your account.

There are times when a Creditor may take money from your wages or your bank account without going through the Court process of obtaining a Judgment and then a Garnishment Summons. Of course, child support enforcement agencies (DCSE) may initiate a wage withholding if you are behind on child support. DCSE may take up to 65% of your pay after taxes for past due child support. The IRS and the Virginia Department of Taxation can also require an employer to withhold money for past due taxes. The IRS can take up to 75 % of your pay after taxes and the Virginia Department of Taxation can take your entire pay check. Guess who wrote the rules on wage withholdings? Monies withheld under these provisions go directly to the agency that has initiated the wage withholding after each pay check.

Another instance that we see frequently in this area of wage withholding without a garnishment is for military members. Many creditors will have a service member sign a form that allows the Creditor to start an involuntary allotment from the service member's pay. They can submit this form directly to DFAS (the agency responsible for military pay and since the service member has signed it, the Creditor does not need to go to court to have the allotment started. Unlike a garnishment where the money is held and then sent to the court on or before the hearing date, involuntary allotments go directly to the creditor after each pay period.

One final instance where a creditor may take money from your bank account without going through the court process is where you have a bank account and a credit account with the same bank or credit union. Virtually every credit union and many banks have provisions in those forms you signed when you opened your accounts that allows them to take money out of your account if you are delinquent on your payments to them. If you have a checking or savings account with a bank or credit union where you also have a loan or credit card that you are having difficulty paying, you should move your money to a new bank or credit union where you do not owe money.

If you are currently being garnished, you need to take immediate action to stop this creditor collection action. You may be able to recover the money that has been withheld if you act quickly enough. Garnishments go in cycles with the creditor adding interest and collection fees every time they collect on a garnishment. If you are involved in the seemingly never ending garnishment cycle, don't despair. You can stop this collection action.

MYTH NUMBER FOUR - THEY WILL TELL MY EMPLOYER, FAMILY OR NEIGHBORS IF I FALL BEHIND ON PAYMENTS.

This is another area where collection agencies frequently use misleading statements to try to coerce individuals to make payments that they can't afford to make. They will tell you that if you don't make a payment, they will have to contact your employer. They may also leave a message saying that if you don't return their call, they will have to contact your neighbors or family members to reach you. These are all methods to intimidate you into making a payment to them. You need to keep in mind that debt collectors are normally paid a commission based on the amount that they collect from individuals. They will try anything that they can think of to make you pay.

I had a client once who received a frantic phone call from her grandmother. The grandmother had received a call from someone who said they were trying to get in touch with my client because they had received information that she had been in an accident and they needed to talk to her about the accident. Did Grandmother know how to get in touch with granddaughter? Granddaughter had not been in an accident and was able to determine that the call was from a creditor. But this shows the lengths that collection agencies will go to in trying to contact an individual.

Under the Fair Debt Collection Practices Act, collection agencies may call neighbors, family members or an employment phone number. However, they may not tell anyone other than the debtor the reason for their call. They cannot mislead anyone as to who is calling by giving a false company name or reason. In addition, while a collection agency can call the debtor at work, they must stop the calls if the debtor tells them that the debtor cannot talk to them at work. There are also limits on the calls made to others. Debt collectors are prohibited from harassing anyone with multiple phone calls during a short period of time.

Unfortunately, many collection agencies ignore the laws that restrict their phone calls. While there can be severe penalties for breaking the laws, most consumers are not aware of their rights. Unscrupulous collection agencies rely on the fact that most consumers will not take action against them and just want the phone calls to stop. They then use this to convince you to make a payment to them.

Many years ago, I handled my son's finances while he was in the military and deployed. He was young and had a few accounts that were past due. I contacted the companies to make payment arrangements. One collection agency that I contacted tried to talk me into paying off the balance of the debt in full to "protect" my son. They said they would have to contact his command if they did not receive the payment. Since I was well aware of the laws governing them and protecting my son during his deployment, I was able to give it back to them as tough as they tried to give it to me. In the end, I paid the bills as I was able to out of my son's pay and when he returned home, he was caught up on his bills. But even though the collection agents knew they were talking to an attorney, they still tried to pressure me into paying off the account immediately.

There are far better options for dealing with collection agencies than giving in to their high pressure tactics that only stall them temporarily. If you are receiving these types of harassing phone calls, you need to take immediate action to end the calls permanently.

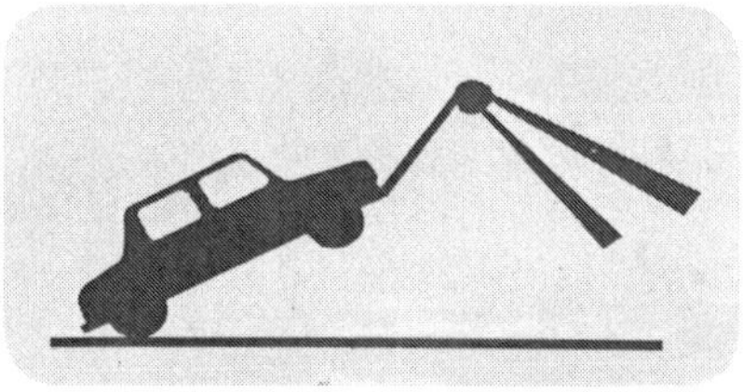

<u>MYTH NUMBER FIVE: IF THEY TAKE MY CAR, I DON'T HAVE TO WORRY ABOUT THE DEBT ANYMORE.</u>

One of the sad facts of life is that sometimes things happen that are out of our control. When an individual faces financial difficulties, they are forced to make tough decisions about what bills to pay. Many times the car payment is pushed aside in order to buy groceries or keep the power on. When you fall behind on your car payments, the creditor will eventually repossess the car. Unfortunately, if you had bad credit and had to take a high interest rate to get the car loan, the creditor will be much quicker to take action when the account falls behind.

After a car is repossessed by the creditor, they must wait 10 days before they can sell the car. During that time, you have the right to "redeem" the car by paying the past due amount. This redemption can be done through a bankruptcy. If the car is not redeemed within the allowed time period, the creditor will sell the car. Normally the car is sold at an auction and the creditor will make little to no effort to attempt to get a fair value for the car. Once the car has been sold, the creditor is supposed to send you a letter detailing the status of the account. They are supposed to tell you how much was owed on the car at the time of the repossession, what fees and expenses they added to the account for the repossession and the auction, and what they received at the auction, the amount left is called the deficiency balance. This is the amount that you still owe the creditor for the car.

Since the creditor sells the car at auction for far less than the fair market value of the car and then adds all sorts of fees and costs on to the balance, it is not unusual for someone to end up owing the creditor more after the sale than they did before the car was repossessed. Car creditors are very quick to go to court and obtain a judgment for the deficiency balance after the sale has been concluded. They will also have your bank information from your payments and probably your employer information from your credit application so they have all the information they need to start garnishing your wages or your bank account.

The situation can be even worse if you co-sign a loan with someone else. Many people believe that the creditor must try to collect from the "primary" person on the account first. This is a misunderstanding of a co-signed loan. If you co-sign a loan with anyone, there is no such thing as a primary and secondary debtor, you are equally liable on the loan. The creditor is free to choose who they want to collect from. Normally the reason for having a co-signor is that the person who wants the loan does not have good enough credit to get the loan on their own. In that case, you can count on the creditor trying to collect from the person who has the better credit.

I recently met with a young lady who had co-signed a car loan with her now ex-boyfriend. The car loan was for his car and they borrowed about $17,000. After they broke up, he stopped making payments on the car and it was repossessed. By the time the creditor went to court for the deficiency judgment, they claimed the balance on the loan was over $22,000. Because she had excellent credit and a decent job, they went after her for the balance on the loan for a car that she never had. Don't let this happen to you.

If you have a car loan and are behind on your payments, you need to take action immediately. There are things that you can do that may help you to lower the car payments and still keep the car, or return the car and walk away from the debt. If you have had a car repossessed in the last week, you must take immediate action if you want to get the car back. Whatever you choose to do about the car, don't rely on statements from the creditor that imply you will not owe anything if they can just get the car back.

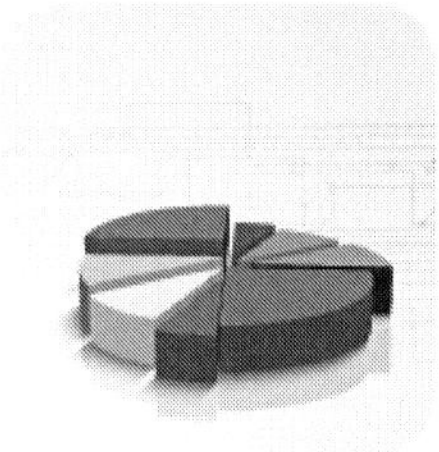

<u>MYTH NUMBER SIX: I CAN'T INCLUDE THIS DEBT IN A BANKRUPTCY.</u>

One of the most common myths I hear regarding filing bankruptcy is that I can't include this debt in my bankruptcy. A varation of this is I don't want to list my house, my car or the loan that I co-signed with my family member in my bankruptcy. When you file bankruptcy, all of your debts and all of your assets must be listed in your bankruptcy. However different types of debts will be treated differently.

There are some debts that cannot be discharged or wiped out in a bankruptcy. These include certain taxes, student loans except in extraordinary circumstances and what is referred to as a Domestic Support Obligation. A Domestic Support Obligation is court ordered support payments such as child support or spousal support. It also includes support payments that are in a valid Separation Agreement. A Domestic Support Obligation may also include a property settlement. There are also a limited number of circumstances where a creditor can ask the Court to declare that the debt owed to them should not be included in the discharge.

While these debts may survive the bankruptcy discharge, they still must be listed in the bankruptcy petition. In addition, bankruptcy can assist you in dealing with these debts. I will discuss taxes in more detail in a later chapter. If you are behind on support payments, you may be able to catch up those payments in a Chapter 13 bankruptcy. In certain circumstances, you may be able to discharge your obligations for a property settlement. While student loans cannot be discharged, except in extreme hardship cases, a bankruptcy may suspend the collection activities on the student loans for a period of time. A bankruptcy may also assist you in clearing other obligations and leave you in a better position to make the payments on a student loan.

Since student loan companies do report to credit reporting agencies, making the payments on a student loan after a bankruptcy is one of the best ways to improve your credit score.

Car loans with a credit unions can also cause individuals hardship after a bankruptcy. Many credit unions have what is referred to as a cross collateralization agreement in their loan agreements. What this means is that if you have a loan that is secured by something, like a car, that collateral secures all debts that you have with that creditor. Credit unions use these agreements regularly to collect on a personal loan or credit card bill after a bankruptcy where the debtor had a car loan with the credit union. While the personal loan or credit card debt was discharged in the bankruptcy, the credit union can refuse to release the title to the car until the other debt has been paid. However, there are ways around this provision in bankruptcy.

If you have debts that may not be discharged in a bankruptcy, you should talk to an experienced bankruptcy attorney about how bankruptcy can help you to deal with your overall debt structure. You may find that a bankruptcy will help you to reach a point where you can deal with those debts that will have to be paid.

MYTH NUMBER SEVEN: I CAN'T FILE BANKRUPTCY BECAUSE ...

I hear many variations on this, from "because I have a security clearance" to "because I will get fired if I file" to " because I won't be able to get a job if I file bankruptcy." While it is true that many employers are doing credit checks on employees especially before hiring a new person, normally what employers are looking for is someone who is a risk. This is one area where bankruptcy can help you to improve your credit report. If you currently have several outstanding credit accounts, you have the potential to be much more likely to have future financial problems that may impact your employment than someone who has filed bankruptcy and cleared up the open credit accounts. Like any other blemishes on your history, it is much better to be open and up front with a prospective employer, if they ask to check your credit history. You can explain that you have filed bankruptcy, the circumstances that lead to your filing and what you have done since you filed to improve your management of your finances.

If your concern is about your current employer, there are protections within the bankruptcy code against discrimination based solely on having filed bankruptcy. The bankruptcy code has a section that prohibits a private employer from terminating or discriminating against an individual solely because that person has filed a bankruptcy or not paid a debt that was discharged in a bankruptcy. The code also has very broad antidiscrimination provisions for individuals employed by any government agency. These provisions not only apply to employees but also to anyone who is seeking license, charter or grant from a government agency with very limited exceptions. There is also a provision that a government agency operating a student loan program cannot deny a student loan solely on the basis of the individual having filed a bankruptcy.

These laws are there to protect an individual from pressure to not file a bankruptcy because they fear losing their job if they file. Society has an interest in allowing individuals to remove the financial pressures that they may be under through a structured process like bankruptcy. We, as a society, have realized that it is far better to allow someone to wipe out debt than to put someone under such severe pressure to repay debts that they will do anything to get the money to repay the debts. Many years ago, society used to throw people into jail when they were unable to repay debts. We, as a society, have come to the understanding that debtor's prisons, as they were called, do not work. It is far more productive to society to keep people in the workforce and remove their debts than to threaten to throw someone into jail for the failure to pay debts.

While bankruptcy filings are public records, just like Judgments, Speeding Tickets and Divorces, the bankruptcy court does not automatically inform your employer that you have filed a bankruptcy. Bankruptcy filings are published in a business newspaper that very few people actually receive. It is possible to search the court records to see if someone has filed bankruptcy but the search has to be done by name or by social security number. There is no way to search to see who has filed a bankruptcy in the last week, month or year. Even a Google search will not normally reveal the bankruptcy filing. There are normally over 20,000 bankruptcies filed each year in Virginia, so it would be extremely time consuming, not to mention boring, for someone to search the court records to see who has filed bankruptcy.

If you file a Chapter 13 bankruptcy, the monthly payments will normally be set up by the court to be a payroll deduction. However, this can be excused under exceptional circumstances such as someone who does the payroll for their employer or a manager of retail store that could be terminated if they have a court ordered deduction.

MYTH NUMBER EIGHT - IF I FILE BANKRUPTCY, IT WILL RUIN MY CREDIT FOREVER.

One of the most common misunderstandings about bankruptcy is the effect it will have on your credit report. One of the most common scare tactics that creditors and collection agencies use is telling people that if they file bankruptcy, they will never be able to get credit again. Variations on this include, "you will never be able to buy (a house) or (a new car) or (get a student loan) if you file a bankruptcy." The previous chapter addressed the ability to obtain a student loan after bankruptcy. This chapter will deal with those other scare tactics.

While bankruptcy is not a positive credit event, it can actually help to improve your credit score. When a creditor looks at your credit report, they are looking at two things. First, they will look at your previous payment history. This is the area where bankruptcy does not normally help the credit score since it shows that the debts were not paid but were discharged in a bankruptcy. However, most people who file bankruptcy are already behind on many payments or have payments that show as being seriously delinquent or sent to collections. Even those individuals who are current on payments up to the point where they decide to file bankruptcy, know that they are no longer able to keep up with the monthly payments.

It is possible to improve this portion of your credit

score very quickly after filing bankruptcy by having payments that are being made on time. I recommend to clients that they get a credit card after filing bankruptcy to help rebuild their credit. This is especially true if the client does not have other debts that they will be paying on after the bankruptcy, like a car loan. The important thing to remember in improving your credit score after a bankruptcy is to use the credit properly. See Chapter 1 if you need a refresher in the proper way to use a credit card.

The second area that a creditor looks at when reviewing your credit report is what is called your income to debt ratio. This is the area where bankruptcy really helps to improve your credit score. The income to debt ratio means that the creditor will look at what your current monthly income is and at how much you owe. If the amount that you owe is too high compared to your monthly income, you will not qualify for the credit despite how good your payment history is. An interesting side note on this is that the creditor not only looks at how much you actually owe on credit cards but the credit limit. Even if you have small balances on credit cards and an excellent payment history, you still may not qualify for credit because you have the ability to owe much more based on the credit limit on the cards.

After you file bankruptcy, the balances on those debts discharged in the bankruptcy is taken to $0. This means that your income to debt ratio will dramatically improve immediately after your discharge. While different creditors will have different standards for new loans or credit, you may find that you will qualify for credit very shortly after your bankruptcy is completed. I always tell my clients that the longer you wait to apply for a loan after your bankruptcy, the better terms you will be able to get, but you will be able to finance a car or get a credit card almost immediately after having filed.

I recently met with a young lady who was sent to me by her father. I had filed a bankruptcy for her father a few years before. She told me that he was able to get a mortgage on a new house about a year after his bankruptcy was completed. The mortgage companies now require waiting about two years after a bankruptcy before they can finance a home purchase, but you will be able to qualify if you keep your credit clean. I have had many clients who have financed the purchase of a car while in a Chapter 13 bankruptcy or immediately after a Chapter 7 discharge. In fact, there are some companies that specialize in loaning money to individuals for the purchase of a car after a Chapter 7 bankruptcy. Again, having a loan that you are making payments on regularly will help to rebuild your credit.

Part of what I do for my clients is pull a copy of their credit report prior to filing bankruptcy. The service that I use lists the estimated current credit score and the estimated credit score one year after having filed. We see increases from a few points to well over a hundred points simply from cleaning up the credit through a bankruptcy. I have also had loan managers refer individuals to me to file a bankruptcy because they cannot qualify the individual for a loan with their current debts listed. After removing those obligations through a bankruptcy, the loan manager will be able to qualify the individual for a new loan.

Another consideration is whether you will even need to be concerned about your credit score for many years. Many of my clients currently have a home that they are current on and reliable cars that they are keeping. They will not need to have any new loans for several years. I also meet with many people who are retired. They have no intentions of buying a house or a new car in the future. They just want to be rid of the credit card debt, and sometimes the medical debt, so they can enjoy their retirement years. The last thing that they are worried about is their future credit score.

Some people look to debt consolidation to solve their financial problems. However, one of the dirty little secrets that the debt consolidation companies may not tell you is that their service can actually do more damage to your credit report than a bankruptcy. Since they negotiate voluntary repayment plans with credit card companies, the credit card companies can, and normally do, report that the account is delinquent according to the original contract. When you couple this with the fact that these companies do not work with medical debt or secured loans, like a mortgage or car loan, your credit may actually worsen while you are in the repayment plan. Instead of being able to begin rebuilding your credit immediately, you will have to finish the payment plan which may go for several years and then start to rebuild your score. This will put you years behind someone who has filed a bankruptcy and is now debt-free.

Myth Number Nine - I will lose my house or my car if I file bankruptcy.

This is another common collection tactic that I have seen used over the years. Collection agent or creditor will tell someone that if they file for bankruptcy they will lose their house or other possessions such as their car. Once again, these dishonest collection agents are twisting the law to attempt to frighten individuals into not seeking advice about how bankruptcy can relieve them of the stress of their debts.

There are basically two types of bankruptcies that individuals file, Chapter 7 and Chapter 13. While individuals can file Chapter 11 bankruptcies, these are normally business reorganizations. A Chapter 7 bankruptcy is actually called a liquidation bankruptcy. In a Chapter 7 case, the Court appoints an individual, called a trustee, to see if there is any way that the debtor's unsecured creditors can be paid. The trustee is not normally concerned about whether car loans or mortgages are going to be paid after the bankruptcy. Their job is to seek ways to pay the unsecured debts, like credit cards, medical, personal loans, etc. In an attempt to find funds to pay these creditors, the trustee will review the things that the debtor owns; like cars, houses, and money in the bank. The trustee will also look at things that the debtor may be entitled to like tax refunds, inheritances, cash value in insurance policies, spousal support or money owed to the debtor. These are called assets.

If the trustee believes that an asset is valuable enough to sell or liquidate, he is obligated to do so to pay something to the creditors. However, in Virginia, the state allows the debtors to protect certain things from the trustee through things called exemptions. There are a number of different exemptions to allow a debtor to keep basic items like household goods, clothing, a car under $6,000 in value, child support payments or arrears, and pets. The law also allows what is normally called a wild card exemption that can be used to protect assets where there is no specific exemption like money in the bank, tax refunds or equity in a home. The amount of wild card exemption that you may be entitled to will be different under different circumstances and you need to consult with an experienced bankruptcy attorney to see what you can protect. In addition, the wild card exemption is a life time exemption in Virginia, so if you have filed a bankruptcy before, you may have used some of your lifetime exemption in the previous case. This will limit the amount that you can claim in a new case.

Another aspect that the trustee will look at is whether there are liens against the property. There are a number of different types of liens. The most common is a mortgage lien on real estate or a lien on a motor vehicle for the loan to purchase the car. If the trustee is going to sell an asset like a house or a car that has a lien on it, he will have to pay off the lien out of the proceeds of the sale. The amount that would be available after the lien is paid is referred to as equity. The trustee will not sell an asset if he feels there is no equity. In other words, if all of the money from a sale would go towards paying off the mortgage or the car loan, the trustee has no interest in selling the house or the car. The trustee will also take into consideration the cost of selling the house or the car. Normally 5 to 10 % of the proceeds from a sale will have to go towards the costs in selling the asset. If there will not be any money left after paying off the liens and the costs of the sale, the trustee will not attempt to sell an asset.

There are times where an individual does have equity in a house, a car or some other asset that can not be protected by the allowed exemptions. In that case, if the individual files a Chapter 7, the trustee's job is to sell or liquidate that asset to pay something to the unsecured creditors. However, an individual may instead file a Chapter 13 bankruptcy to protect an asset. The Chapter 13 bankruptcy is a repayment plan. When a Chapter 13 bankruptcy is filed to protect an asset, you will need to have a liquidation test prepared. This is a formula that estimates how much money would be available to unsecured creditors if it were a Chapter 7 case. The debtor may then propose a plan to pay the creditors at least that much through a Chapter 13 repayment plan over a three to five year period. This allows the debtor to keep the asset and prevent a liquidation.

A second way that an individual could lose a house or a car in bankruptcy is if they are behind on the payments. If you are not current on your mortgage payments or on your car payments and file a Chapter 7 bankruptcy, the creditor may choose to take the house or the car back. There is no way to prevent that in a Chapter 7 bankruptcy. However, if you are behind on your car payments or your mortgage, you can instead file a Chapter 13 bankruptcy to catch up what you are behind and keep your house or your car. If you are behind on your mortgage payments and/or your car payments and want to keep the house and/or the car, you need to contact an experienced bankruptcy attorney as quickly as possible so they can evaluate your circumstances. The longer you wait the more expensive it will be to save your house and/or your car.

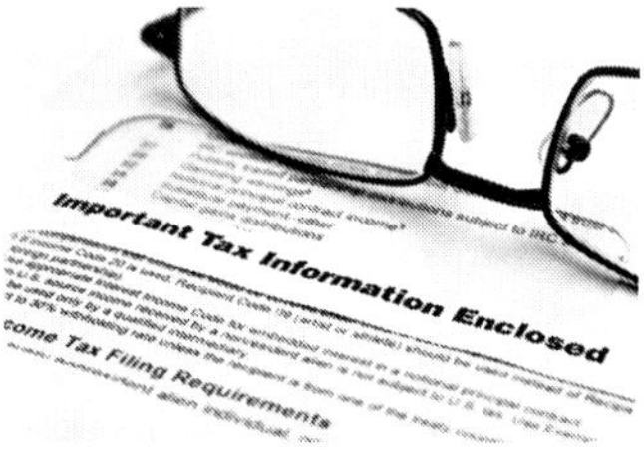

MYTH NUMBER TEN - BANKRUPTCY WON'T HELP ME BECAUSE I OWE TAXES.

This is another one of the things I hear from clients who have been told by their friend, relative or even their accountant, that bankruptcy won't help them because they owe back taxes. Like many of the other issues that I have discussed in this book, there is some truth to this, but it is also misleading. Taxes can fall into several different categories in bankruptcy.

The first category of tax debt deals with income taxes as determined by your tax returns. After you have filed all tax returns, an experienced bankruptcy attorney will be able to determine what category your taxes fall into. For three years after a tax return is due, the tax is called a priority debt and can not be discharged in bankruptcy. However the penalties and interest on that tax debt may be able to be discharged in a bankruptcy. The three years runs from the date that the tax returns were required to be filed including any extensions that have been granted. This would normally be April 15th for Federal Taxes and May 1st for State Taxes but if you request an extension on or before the filing date, you are normally given until October 15th to file the Federal Tax Returns. The three years would then run from the date of the extension or from October 15th.

The three year rule only applies if the tax returns were timely filed. If the tax returns were not filed on time, then for two years after the tax returns were filed, the taxes are not dischargeable in bankruptcy. In addition, the IRS or the state may do an assessment of taxes either when tax returns are filed or when they are reviewed for some reason. Taxes are not dischargeable for 240 days after the assessment.

These tax debts will survive a Chapter 7 bankruptcy. However, you can pay the taxes back through a structured repayment plan in a Chapter 13 bankruptcy. The "priority" tax debt will be paid back over a three to five year period. In addition, these taxes are paid back without further penalties or interest on the tax debt. This can save you hundreds of dollars if you have a large tax debt.

Another consideration, if you live in Hampton Roads, is that you must have filed all tax returns that you are required to file before your bankruptcy is filed with the court or very shortly there after. There is a standard policy here that if you file a Chapter 13 bankruptcy and have not filed all required tax returns, your case will be dismissed. In a Chapter 7 bankruptcy, the case is not normally dismissed but it will be held open until all required tax returns have been filed. In addition, if you have not filed tax returns for a year before filing a Chapter 7 bankruptcy, any taxes owed for that year are not dischargeable regardless of when the tax return should have been filed.

After the applicable time period, the taxes may be discharged in bankruptcy. However, the IRS or the State may protect itself from discharge and initiate collection action by filing a tax lien. The tax lien then attaches to all property that the individual owns to include money in the bank and wages. Several years ago, the IRS conducted a tax liquidation auction on Willie Nelson's property due to unpaid taxes. They sold everything that he owned to pay off the tax debt. If you own real estate, the tax lien will attach to your real estate and must be paid to transfer the real estate.

The IRS or the state can also attempt to collect the taxes owed by issuing a tax lien and wage garnishment against your wages. If the IRS sends the tax lien to your employer, they must withhold 75% of your income for the tax debt. Unlike other garnishments, this lien will remain in place until the taxes are paid in full. If the State sends the tax lien to your employer, they take 100% of your pay check until the taxes are paid in full. In addition, unlike other garnishments that are done through a court with the garnished funds being sent to the court, money withheld under tax liens goes straight to the agency that issued the tax lien. This means that this money cannot be recovered after it is withheld like other garnished funds.

If you have a tax lien, you can stop the IRS or the state from taking your property, to include wages, by filing a bankruptcy. In a Chapter 7 bankruptcy, the IRS or the state will have to stop the collection action while you are in bankruptcy but they can continue to collect on the tax debt after the completion of your case with some exceptions. However, in Chapter 13 bankruptcy, this tax debt can be paid back as part of your bankruptcy plan as a secured debt. Since the tax lien is attached to everything you own, the value of the tax lien is determined by the value of all your assets. You then pay the IRS or the state back an amount equal to the value of all your assets with interest. This can save you hundreds, if not thousands, of dollars. I recently had a case where the individual owed approximately $75,000 in taxes but had only about $15,000 in assets. I put him into a Chapter 13 where he will pay the IRS the $15,000 plus 4% interest over a five year period and wipe out close to $60,000 in tax debt.

Another type of tax debt is property taxes owed to city or county for real estate or for personal property, normally the taxes on your motor vehicle. This tax cannot be discharged for one year after it is due. However, in Virginia, property taxes attach to the item that the taxes is for and become secured debt. The city or county has the right to sell your house or your car to pay back taxes that are owed on it. This debt can also be paid back through a Chapter 13 bankruptcy and is paid without penalty or interest. If you are behind on your real estate or personal property taxes, you can protect your house or car by filing a Chapter 13 bankruptcy. If you no longer have the car, you can discharge personal property taxes that are over a year old.

The final category of taxes that I will address in this book are taxes that you were supposed to collect for the government. This is normally sales taxes or income withholding taxes that you were required to collect and pay as an employer. These taxes are never dischargeable in bankruptcy. Like income taxes and property taxes, these taxes may be paid back through a Chapter 13 bankruptcy.

Conclusion

I hope this book has helped you to understand debt collection and bankruptcy better. While the information contained in this book is general in nature, these types of actions will normally follow similar paths. It is my desire that you become better informed about your options when dealing with debts.

If you feel that the best option for you at this point is a bankruptcy, please give us a call at 757-340-3100. My associate or I will be happy to meet with you to discuss how a bankruptcy can help you in your particular situation. Just as no two individuals will have identical debts, no two bankruptcies will be identical. You need to know how we can help you to improve your life by removing the burden of debt that you can not afford to repay or by dealing with financial issues like mortgage arrears or tax debts.

The worst thing that you can do in dealing with financial issues is to do nothing and hope things will improve in the future. You must be proactive in handling your debts. Putting things off will only make matters worse. Whether you decide to file a bankruptcy, deal directly with your creditors or work with a debt consolidation company, you need to take action immediately.

Call us today to see how we can relieve you of the stress you are currently feeling and join the thousands of individuals that we have helped to become debt free.

TESTIMONIALS

"[M]ade a difficult person situation for me so much less stressful."
-Mary from Virginia Beach, Va.

"Got the job done effectively and affordably."
-Tina from Portsmouth, Va.

"Ms. Pfeiffer was very knowledgeable and very helpful on any questions I had."
-Bill from Virginia Beach, Va.

"She treated me with kindness and respect before, during, and after the entire process was complete."
-Daynean from Portsmouth, Va.

"She got me through this awful debt process without me totally losing my mind!"
-Kathy from Virginia Beach, Va.

"Very professional. Knows how to get things done"
-Harry & Debby from Chesapeake, Va.

"Everything [Ms. Pfeiffer] told me was true and made my case go with ease."
-Nadine from Virginia Beach, Va.

"Efficient service with detailed explanation of the bankruptcy process. Having all my questions answered at every step of the process allowed me to proceed

with confidence."
-Anon.

"The help, advice, and guidance made our experience almost painless."
-Anon.

"Very helpful in explaining the procedures and laws concerning Bankruptcy."
-Anon.

"Mrs. Pfeiffer was excellent at explaining everything so that I could understand it. She was kind and patient, very thorough and professional."
-Anon.

"Edrie Pfeiffer helped take the stress out of our Bankruptcy."
-Anon.

ABOUT THE AUTHOR

Edrie Pfeiffer grew up in a rural area in Eastern Oregon in a blue collar family. While her family never had a lot, they never went hungry, since they owned a small farm where they grew most of their own food. Her father had a small business delivering dairy products to grocery stores, restaurants and other businesses. After being a stay at home mother for many years, Edrie's mother went to college while Edrie was in middle and high school. After obtaining a degree, she taught kindergarten for a few years before retiring.

Her parents' example instilled a strong work ethic in Edrie and taught her the benefit of good customer service. She was expected to help out on the farm and also worked from the time she was old enough to have a paper route. Her family encouraged a well rounded life with music lessons, dance lessons and sports activities. In High School, Edrie was on the Drill Team and sang in the choir. She was also active in her church, showing her independent nature by deciding in middle school to join a different church than her parents attended.

Edrie went to Oregon State University for her Bachelor's degree. While at OSU, she joined Kappa Delta Sorority and served in several different officer positions, to include serving as President of the sorority her last year in school. Edrie also chose to participate in ROTC and was one of the student leaders in this program. She received several awards in the ROTC program and after receiving her degree, she was commissioned as an officer in the

United States Army.

While serving in the Army, Edrie was stationed in several different places from Ft. Lee, Virginia, to El Paso, Texas to Tooele, Utah. She also spent a year in Korea. During her time in Texas, she managed to complete a two year Master's degree program in one year. Then while she was stationed in Utah, she met the man that would become her husband. After she left the military, they moved to Virginia to be closer to his family in North and South Carolina.

After working in several different positions, Edrie decided to return to school once again and seek a law degree. She went to Regent University so that she would be able to commute from their home in Newport News. While at Regent, Edrie served on the Law Review and graduated Magna Cum Laude. She then went to Georgetown University School of Law and obtained a Master of Law graduating with distinction, again completing a two year program in one year.

During law school, Edrie worked for a local firm that handled bankruptcies. She saw how bankruptcy could assist people in overcoming terrible financial situations. After helping several clients through the difficult process, Edrie knew that she had found her calling and has worked in the bankruptcy field ever since. She feels fortunate to be able to assist people who are going through tough times and are trying to improve their situation.

Edrie joined the Law Office of Martin Garfinkel in

January of 2001 and became his partner in 2003. When Mr. Garfinkel retired in 2005, Edrie took over the practice and changed the name to Hampton Roads Legal Services. She and her husband moved to Virginia Beach in 2007 and have lived in the local area since then. They are active in their church and other community affairs. Edrie is especially drawn to working with at risk children and has served as a Big Sister and a Foster Parent.

NOTES: